AN INTERNATIONAL EDUCATIONAL EXPERIENCE

DR PROSPER K ZIGAH

KINDLE DIRECT PUBLISHING

Copyright © 2024 KINDLE DIRECT PUBLISHING

All rights reserved

The characters and events portrayed in this book are non-fictional. First names are used to reference friends in most cases.

No part of this book may be reproduced, or stored in a retrieval system, or transmitted in any form or by any means, electronic, mechanical, photocopying, recording, or otherwise, without express written permission of the publisher.

ISBN: 9798340371546

Printed in the United States of America

This book is dedicated to my children Ian Landon Zigah and Ivan Carter Zigah.

FOREWORD

International students are very important for Universities all over the world. They increase diversity on campus. They enrich intellectual discourse. They also add to the revenue of academic institutions through payment of fees and other charges.

Increasingly, more academic institutions are embarking on activities to attract and retain talented international students and faculty. At the same time, several nations are also investing resources to retain their talented scientists, researchers and students.

In the USA and Europe, the number of international students keep increasing. In the Netherlands, international students account for a considerable fraction of the student population.

Having an international education is highly valuable and desired by many nations and academic institutions. It is also very important for students, teachers, educators and educational administrators. It broadens perspectives on discussions of human growth, social interactions, political activities, economic progress and technological and developmental needs.

As a beneficiary of international education, I am happy to share some of my experiences in this book. This book is a nonfictional account of my time at Wageningen University from 2003-2005.

This book will be a great read for students, professors, parents, counselors, educators and researchers.

This book will also be a good resource if you are trying to access international education, recruit international students, staff and faculty, address diversity or retain international personnel.

AN INTERNATIONAL EDUCATIONAL EXPERIENCE

BY

DR PROSPER K. ZIGAH

CHAPTER ONE

FELLOWSHIP TO STUDY ABROAD

At the tail end of my national service at the school of Agriculture, University of Cape Coast, I received a fellowship from the Netherlands Fellowship Program (NFP) to pursue a master of science degree in Environmental Science at the prestigious Wageningen University.

The fellowship covers transportation to the school and from Wageningen at the end of the study program. It also includes monthly payments for subsistence to the fellows.

My friend and office mate Moses was also awarded a similar fellowship (Wageningen University fellowship - WUF) for a master's study at the same school. David was also awarded a fellowship by Wageningen few months later for a master's degree program.

CHAPTER TWO

WAGENINGEN UNIVERSITY

Wageningen University is a prestigious research University in the Netherlands.

It is one of the top Universities in the field of Life Sciences .

The University was ranked as number 3 in the Netherlands and number 64 in the world in the 2024 Times Higher Education World University Ranking.

In the Life Sciences, the school was ranked as number 19 in the world in the 2024 Times Higher Education World University Ranking.

CHAPTER THREE

TRIP TO THE NETHERLANDS

Around August 2003, I received details of my travel from the University in an email correspondence. Two weeks later I was ready for my trip to Wageningen. I flew to Schiphol Airport at Amsterdam in the Netherlands.

On arrival, I met other students from Africa who were also heading to Wageningen. There were a lot of traffic at the train station. We were alerted by one of the students that we should be careful because he was told they do steal things at train station.

We bought our train tickets from the ticketing counter to Wageningen. Soon the train arrived. We boarded the train at Amsterdam to Arnhem. One student lost one of his bags. We think it was stolen. I had two pieces of traveling bags. One was filled with my clothes and other personal effects. The other was filled with food items like Shito, Tin fish and Gari.

Other students had mostly 2 or 3 pieces of luggage.

Some of the other students from Ghana were Felix, Razak, Sally, Martin, and Teressa.

At Arnhem, we took a connector to Ed-Wageningen. And another bus to Wageningen University.

CHAPTER FOUR

ARRIVAL AT WAGENINGEN UNIVERSITY

We met a foreign student's officer at the Administration building. He was a Nigerian. A really nice gentleman. He greeted us. And nicely asked if we wanted a glass of water or a glass of juice.

I opted for a glass of juice. To be honest, I actually wanted water and then juice. Most of the other students asked for a glass of juice as well.

Soon later, I asked for a glass of water. Other students also asked for water. He chuckled. Then fetched and served us the glasses of water.

You know, in Ghana, you are typically offered water after a long trip. Then drinks. Then food, depending on the host.

The Officer went through the initial welcome formalities with us. Then led us into another room to meet the Dutch foreign students' representative.

She presented each of us with folders containing information about the school and the city. Also included was our assigned hall of residence.

CHAPTER FIVE

HALL OF RESIDENCE AND CORRIDOR MEMBERS

I was placed in the Dijkgraaf Hall. Another student Razak was placed at the same hall.

We were given rides in a car to our halls and were given keys to our rooms. My room was a typical student room with study desk and chair. And a comfortable bed. Bathroom was shared.

We also had a big kitchen for all the corridor (floor) members. There are about 10 students per corridor. In addition to myself and Razak, we had one Italian student, and about 5 Dutch students on our corridor.

Fortunately, we had really nice corridor mates. By all account a great group of students. Over the next year, we bonded and played games.

We agreed on a cooking schedule. We took turns to prepare meals for the group. Whoever cooks does not do the dishes. Another student was assigned to do dishes. We also bought crates of Dutch or European beers each week. I got the chance to learn a lot about the Dutch culture from my corridor mates. We went out sometimes. There is a bunker bar at the hall for the students to drink, dance and socialize.

CHAPTER SIX

A LITTLE BIT ABOUT THE DUTCH AND DUTCH STUDENTS

One thing that stuck with me all these years was the Dutch saying that "There are three Ws you can not trust'. The Ws were work, weather and women.

Another was the washing of dishes without rinsing off the soap. Lastly is making sure all the dishes were well dried before putting them away.

I once asked my good old Dutch friend why don't you rinse off the soap. He laughed and responded. Ah, that is not necessary here in Holland. Our soaps are phosphorus free.

It turned out that before we arrived, the Dutch had few years ago passed a directive that mandated the use of phosphate free soaps. So washing plates and cutlery only involved one-step. In soapy water. Then dried fully on the dryer or with a kitchen towel.

The Dutch students also drink beers a lot. We picked up this pretty quickly. We went through about 4-6 crates (~ 48 to 72 pieces) of beers a week. These were for all of us on the corridor.

The Dutch are the tallest people on the planet. Historically (since 1950s), they have been the tallest in the world for a very long time. The students I met at Wageningen from the Netherlands were also taller than the rest of the students. Both the male and female Dutch students were pretty tall.

Typical lunch for the Dutch students I met was a homemade sandwich. Usually with cheese (European cheese) alone or with a choice of meat.

At Wageningen, the Dutch students also leave school around mid-day on Friday for the weekend. To spend the weekend days with family and friends.

They are also athletic looking and muscular.

They by far speak very good English than most nonnative speakers. I have always wondered why this was the case.

Most students ride bikes to and from school. Both the Dutch students and foreign students.

Some students had private cars on campus. But biking was the predominant mode of transport among the students. I rode my bike about 20 minutes to get to lecture halls.

CHAPTER SEVEN

CLASSES

All my courses at Wageningen were taught in English. This was great for us as most of the international graduate students at the time neither spoke or could write in Dutch.

We had smaller number of students in our classes.

We had good mix of Dutch and international students in all my classes. Students were from Peru, Nepal, France, China, Ghana, Nigeria, Gambia, Zimbabwe, Ethiopia, Uganda, Australia, Germany etcetera.

Most of the students co-existed nicely in most of the classes.

CHAPTER EIGHT

PERIOD BASED, NON-SEMESTER ACADEMIC YEAR

At Wageningen, the academic year is not divided into two semesters. The academic year is divided into 6 teaching periods.

Each period lasted approximately two months. Two courses per period is typical.

There is an examination at the end of the period.

CHAPTER NINE

COURSE CASE STUDIES

Several case studies in the courses we took required us to form study groups.

I was in the Environmental Systems Analysis group. Most of my courses were on Environmental systems analysis, Environmental measurements, and Environmental and Natural resources management and policy.

Among my initial courses was the module Environmental Measurement. This module included several homework problems and a case study.

Another interesting class was Environmental economics and policy. Part of the class was completing a modeling assignment. My study group mate was an Ethiopian. My good old friend Solomon. We met regularly to work on the model development and complete the assignment.

Natural resources management was another interesting class. In this module, we completed many homework problems and a case study. My study group mate was a Nepali student Santosh. We met daily after lunch to work on the problems. Santosh had a strong math background which helped a lot in solving these home works. Santosh and I became good friends off class as well. We played ping pong at the gym few times a week.

CHAPTER TEN

CASE STUDY ON GREAT BARRIER REEF

A part of the module Environmental Systems Analysis required us to complete a case study. We were to do this in groups. Matt, jasmine, Linda, Sophie and myself constituted the study group for this case study.

This was an interesting group in terms of diversity. Matt is from Australia. I was from Ghana. Jasmine was from USA. Linda was from The Netherlands. Sophie was from France.

We chose the Great Barrier Reef system in Australia as our project topic. We researched aspects of the reef system for this case study.

The group dynamic was very enriching. Perspectives are pretty divergent on most issues. We got to know each other well. We worked on various aspects of the case study independently. And then usually one of us, Jasmine, will volunteer to put all the pieces together into a whole report.

She then passes the report to the rest of the group for comments. We then work on the final presentation in a similar fashion. All of us took turns in presenting the work to the class.

Almost all the time, this was well received. We all became good friends in class and off class. We met sometimes for parties and course related discussions.

The last time I spoke to Matt was during my PhD in Minnesota. He was back at Wageningen.

CHAPTER ELEVEN

GYMNASIUM

I went to the school gymnasium three or four times a week. My routine included short running on the treadmill followed by weight lifting. And then playing ping pong with my friend Santosh. At few times we played squash.

Santosh is very good at Ping Pong. I am pretty good at Ping Pong as well. We played at a competitive level all the time. I think we were even on the number of wins.

I built muscle enough to become a bit bulky and fit and did attract some attention.

Later, another friend Nana (Kufuor) and I went to the gym regularly to workout.

CHAPTER TWELVE

RAW CHICKEN EGG AND MILK MIXTURE

An unusual habit I picked up during my intensive gym times was drinking raw eggs with both the egg white and yoke well mixed in whole milk.

This was my protein supplement for a long time.

Initially the taste was not that pleasant but I did enjoy it for a while.

CHAPTER THIRTEEN

BASEBALL CAP

I soon started wearing baseball cap all the time. The habit started during my last year in Africa and continue at Wageningen. I started having receding hairline during my last year in Africa. I was then a teaching assistant at the University of Cape Coast where I got my bachelor's degree.

Initially putting on the cap was I guess to conceal the hairline.

Later, I became fascinated with having the cap on to the point that whenever the cap was off, it felt awkward.

I had the cap on most of the time at Wageningen. Both in class and off class settings.

It was easy to make me out because the Dutch and other European students hardly had this cap-wearing habit or dress-style.

Few times I have had colleagues and teachers wonder why I still had the cap on after a haircut or during in-class work.

Some just assumed I was American at the time. I was surprise to learn that some of my friends taught I spoke like an American.

This went on for about a year until I went to Florida in the fall of 2004 for a 6-month internship.

In Florida, I soon discovered that even in the USA, most Americans hardly had the cap on that much. Certainly, the use of baseball cap was way more common in the USA than in the Netherlands.

A key difference for me while in the USA was that no one asked me or wondered why I had the cap on. Admittedly, I only had the cap on after work during my internship.

Most of my colleague interns and other workers at the Company I worked for in Florida did not put cap on during work or even after work.

My use of the baseball cap subsequently declined. I kept the habit on low key after I returned to the Netherlands to continue my studies.

CHAPTER FOURTEEN

SOCCER

Some students at Wageningen met regularly to play soccer. Once or twice a week. After class hours 7-9 pm was the best times for soccer.

Most of the Ghana students in the soccer team were Moses, David, Samuel, myself, Ben, Francis (Old Soldier), Marfo, Asare, Balma, Hearzy, Peter and John. Some were PhD students like Peter and John. Most of us were master's students.

I have above average soccer skills. By far, I was one of the good soccer players in the group. Soccer was so much fun for us. Few times we had competitive games.

We played games against other soccer teams at Wageningen. Our soccer team was part of the intramural soccer competition at Wageningen.

But for the most part, we split into smaller groups and played noncompetitive games.

We also had a soccer coach. He lived in the city of Wageningen but was not a student. He trained us well. We did a lot of running and other exercises to condition ourselves for games.

Soccer was great for us. We needed it to release stress and also get to know each other. And to be in good physical shape as well.

CHAPTER FIFTEEN

PARTIES

We organize regular house parties at Wageningen. During my first year, most of the parties were hosted by the PhD students who had been in residence for a while. Peter, John, Francis and Ben hosted few parties for us.

Typically, the host will cook and buy some drinks to share. Then ask the attending students to also bring drinks and desserts to share with the group.

A times, the host will ask the attending students come early and help prepare the meal.

There were several ladies among us at the time. Some were Sally, Teressa, Betty and Joana.

Songs that are played during the parties were mostly selected by the host. Most of the songs were Ghana hiplife, Ghana highlife, R&B, Hippop, and Reggae songs.

Dressing at the parties was casual. Dancing usually commences after eating dinner and socializing a bit.

Most people dance at the parties. From the beginning of playing songs to the end.

Sometimes, we continue the parties in town. Especially when the party is on Friday night or over the weekends. It is common for some of the PhDs to bring few of us with to town to continue the party. We also used the bunker bar at Dijkgraaf hall and the bar at the Bornsesteg hall to continue partying.

We tended to socialize at the bars or during parties. It is common for a male student to grab a female student's hand and ask for a dance. Most did accept and danced.

If the party did extend to the city center, we also socialize with the other residents or students. Heartily chatting with them or dancing with them. Several students from out of town and local nonstudent residents come to the city of Wageningen for parties.

I met some friends from nearby towns during some of these parties.

CHAPTER SIXTEEN

VACATIONS IN LONDON

The Netherlands is few hours by air from London in England. During school recess after end of period examination, I usually flew to London to visit my good friend Nathaniel.

I tended to flew cheap using either EasyJet or RyanAir. The visit usually lasted one to two weeks.

Nathaniel and I knew each other back during our secondary school days. We both attended the same secondary school - West Africa Secondary School.

Nathaniel studied Chemistry at College. He then studied Pharmacy in London during those times. He is now a Pharmacist in England.

I was able to visit London to two or three times during my study at Wageningen. We lived at Southwest London city of Mitcham. And later at Northwest London city of Camden Town.

We had so much fun during my visits. We toured various attractions in London. We cooked good Ghanaian meals.

We visited many mutual friends who were also living in London. I had few friends visit me while in London. I met new friends through Nathaniel as well.

Nathaniel's friend at the time Millie was a nice lady. She and her family played great host during my visit.

During one of my visits to London, I traveled north of England to visit a friend from college at Bradford. Laurent was a Graduate student at Bradford University.

Laurent and I were both Teaching Assistants at the University of Cape Coast for one year prior to traveling abroad for graduate studies.

I was in Bradford for several days. While there, we also visited the city of Leeds.

We enjoyed really good food during my visit including our delicacy Banku with Tilapia and ground pepper.

CHAPTER SEVENTEEN

EXCURSION TO THE ATOMIUM IN BRUSSELS

We went on a student excursion to Brussels during my time at Wageningen. Myself, Moses and David were all part of this school trip. We went together with many Wageningen students.

Our tour bus arrived in Brussels late in the afternoon. We were led to the big square at the city center. We had dinner at a restaurant there. We were served with chocolate mousse. Really delicious.

We later toured a chocolate factory in Brussels. We were informed that a huge amount of the chocolate came from Ghana.

We visited the Atomium in Brussels. The Atomium is a key tourist attraction in the city of Brussels. I manage to walk up all the atoms in the giant structure.

We also visited the Jeanneke Pis Statue in Brussels. Portraying a peeing little girl.

Later some of us the students went to the bar to party. A lot of chatting, drinking and socializing.

We left for Wageningen the next day. It was a fun-filled trip.

CHAPTER EIGHTEEN

TRIPS TO AMSTERDAM

I visited Amsterdam several times during my studies at Wageningen. The trip was 1 hour and 2o minutes by train.

Some of the key attraction I went to see were the Red-Light District and some famous coffee shops.

We did shop at several places in Amsterdam. We tended to leave Wageningen in the morning and return on the last train back to Wageningen at night.

There are several concerts in Amsterdam during the summer months. This tend to attract a lot of the students to Amsterdam. I did go to a few of these concerts.

I used the Tram for commute within Amsterdam during my visits.

CHAPTER NINETEEN

CASHLESS TRANSACTIONS

I was introduced to cashless transactions at Wageningen. I went without cash for months at times. No ATM withdrawal of euros for few months.

This is because you really do not need cash on the school campus. All purchases were via a student card.

All the vendors on campus accepted the card. All copiers, printers and book shops did accept the card.

This was an interesting change for most of the international students that were used to paying for things with paper money all the time.

CHAPTER TWENTY

LUNCH

I ate a lot of sandwiches for lunch during my stay at Wageningen. I made these at home.

I made either the cheese sandwich or meat sandwich and bring it with me to school.

There are also plenty options for hot meals at several locations across campus.

CHAPTER TWENTY ONE

DINNER

Since we had a corridor cooking schedule, we ate good food year-round at Wageningen. We prepared good meals for our corridor members.

Our Dutch corridor mates made really delicious Dutch meals for us. I also made really good Ghanaian food for the corridor mates when it was my turn to cook. Our Italian corridor mate made some great Italian food for us as well.

Sometimes I bought and cooked fish pizza for myself. This was one of my favorite food from the grocery store at Wageningen.

There was also a asian restaurant near our hall of residence that I bought food from frequently.

CHAPTER TWENTY TWO

CHURCH SERVICE

I did participate in church activities during my time at Wageningen. I was a member of the International Christian Fellowship at Wageningen University.

We had members from all over the world with different Christianity backgrounds and traditions. I met and became friends with several great people from this church.

Most of the members were part of Wageningen University. But we also had members from outside the school. We met for church services on Sundays.

During our time, we happen to have a Ghanaian as one of the pastors of the church. His name is Pastor Samson. He also graduated from Wageningen University.

CHAPTER TWENTY THREE

INTERNSHIP IN FLORIDA

I completed my internship in Florida. I worked with the company Southern Data Stream Inc. for 6 months. The Southern Data Stream is an environmental consulting firm based in south Florida. The leader is Dr. John Capece.

I enjoyed the internship at Southern Data Stream. There were other interns from India, France, Ghana, Cameroon, Germany, Venezuela and the USA.

Part of my research activities at the company was to collect environmental samples, both water and plants samples and analyzed these at the laboratory. We collected both surface water samples and groundwater samples.

We installed and programmed ISCO autosamplers for collecting the water samples during baseflows and also during peak flows when there is a rainfall event.

The water and vegetative samples collected are usually analyzed at a laboratory at the University of Florida.

I was active in several projects at the company during my

internship.

I met other interns whilst working with Southern Data Stream. They were Sanjay, Sid, Aurelie, Patricia, Isaac, Charlie, Eliane and others.

We traveled around Florida a lot during my internship. We went to different places of attraction in the state on weekends.

We visited the Everglades National Park in Homestead, Florida. We also went to the Walt Disney World in Orlando, Florida.

We did visit the Florida Keys at Archipelago in Florida. And we also traveled to The Kennedy Space Center on Merritt Island in Florida.

We also played soccer, watched movies and visited several restaurants and pubs. We had so much fun in Florida.

There were few storms and a major hurricane during my internship in Florida.

There was one time when we were required to retrieve time sensitive samples from the field. About the same time, we had weather alert on our blackberry phones that our direction will take us right into the middle of the storm.

It was a difficult decision to make since the samples were required by an important client of the firm. After some consultation, our team lead decided we should have a go at retrieving the samples.

So we headed out in the rain. Our driver had both fingers tight on the steering wheel. Visibility was very low. So we drove very slowly.

One of us had to keep an eye on the Blackberry for alerts. The alerts came in constantly giving details of the road condition and weather situation in the path ahead of us.

Once in a while we paused and packed for some time if the alert required so. Few interns made phone calls to families back home and remained on the phone for a long time.

Most of the vehicles we met on the way were heading the opposite direction. Away from the storm.

Eventually we got to the sampling site and retrieved the samples. We cautiously drove back to the office. The samples were then prepped and stored away, ready to go for laboratory analyses.

On another occasion, the interns served as volunteers for political campaigns in the then upcoming elections in November 2004.

We helped political parties' erect posters, give out information leaflets and also encourage drivers and other residents to register and vote. Some of us also held political placards along the streets to campaign for political parties.

We served as volunteers in a bike race and also a local marathon. We were placed at various locations along the biking or running route to give out water bottles to the bikers or runners.

At one time, we were given tickets by our company to watch the University of Florida's Gators football game. The game was at the Ben Hill Griffin Stadium in Gainesville, Florida.

It was a home game for the gators. For most of us interns that was our first time watching a live American football.

From the beginning to end the game was very entertaining. We bought food and drinks and really enjoyed the game.

All too soon, it was time to leave for the Netherlands.

My internship ended and I left for Wageningen to continue my studies.

CHAPTER TWENTY FOUR

RESEARCH AT INTERNATIONAL WATER MANAGEMENT INSTITUTE

International Water Management Institute (IWMI) is a scientific research organization with several offices around the globe. One of the organization's objective is the sustainable use of water and land resources in agriculture.

I visited IWMI in Accra in Ghana for few months. The head of IWMI, Ghana at the time was Dr. Pay Drechsel.

I went to IWMI to collect data for my master's thesis. My thesis project was on evaluating the economic impact of the practice of using wastewater for vegetable farming in Accra.

While there I had the opportunity to attend several conferences and meetings at the Accra office location. I had the rare opportunity to interact with several scientists who are working on various aspects of urban agriculture.

One of the scientists I met was Raymond. Raymond is an old friend from Casely Hayford Hall at the University of Cape Coast. I also met and interacted with the scientists

George, Ben and Philip.

For my research, we visited and interviewed several urban vegetable farmers in the city of Accra. Based on the initial responses, surveys were designed and administered to collect information for the economic analyses.

Data from the surveys allowed us to determine the benefits and costs associated with this urban agricultural practice. We were also able to get a good sense of the potential changes in the livelihoods of these urban farmers should there be a policy change regarding this farming practice.

A thesis report on the economics of urban agriculture was produced. The data was presented to the department upon return to Wageningen University.

I graduated with a master's degree in Environmental Science from Wageningen University in 2005.

THE END

ABOUT THE AUTHOR

Dr Prosper K Zigah

Dr. Prosper Zigah is the President and CEO of PKZ Climate Institute. He is the author of the 2 books "Life at West Africa Secondary School: A memoir of a secondary school education experience" and "Life at the University of Cape Coast: A memoir of tertiary education experience". He is a scientist and a teacher. He holds professional certificates from Harvard University and University of Cambridge. He completed his Doctor of Philosophy degree (PhD) at the University of Minnesota. He holds two master's degrees from Wageningen University and the University of Nottingham. He got his bachelor's degree from the University of Cape Coast.

Dr Zigah was recently a visiting Assistant Professor of Chemistry in the Department of Chemistry, Biochemistry and Physics at Georgia Southern University. Prior to that, he held research scientist positions at Swiss Federal

Institute of Aquatic Science and Technology, Woods Hole Oceanographic Institution and the University of Pittsburgh.

Dr Zigah has been a visiting researcher at Harvard University, University of Massachusetts Amherst, National Ocean Sciences Accelerator Mass Spectrometry Facility, University of Florida and the International Water Management Institute.

Dr Zigah has two lovely boys Ian Landon Zigah and Ivan Carter Zigah. He has lived and worked in several US states including Florida, Maryland, Minnesota, Massachusetts, Pennsylvania and Georgia. He has also lived and worked in the Netherlands, United Kingdom and Switzerland. In his free time, Dr Zigah enjoys hiking, jogging, traveling, cooking, watching soccer, watching football, and writing.

BOOKS BY THIS AUTHOR

Life At The University Of Cape Coast From 1998 To 2002: A Memoir Of Tertiary Education Experience

This is a non-fiction book detailing the experiences I had during my college years at the University of Cape Coast from 1998 to 2002.

Life At West Africa Secondary School From 1994 To 1996: A Memoir Of A Secondary School Education Experience

This book is a non-fictional account of my secondary education at West Africa Secondary School (WASS) from 1994 to 1996.

Made in the USA
Columbia, SC
15 November 2024